Making Dress-Up Games with Phaser v2

Game Starter Kit Course using Phaser v2 Gaming Frameworks

By Stephen Gose

Making Dress-UP Browser Games with Phaser v2

A Starter Kit Course for Dress-up Fashions Game Mechanics

Stephen Gose

This book is for sale at http://leanpub.com/courses/leanpub/mbg-dressup-p2

This version was published on 2018-08-04

This is a Leanpub book. Leanpub empowers authors and publishers with the Lean Publishing process. Lean Publishing is the act of publishing an in-progress ebook using lightweight tools and many iterations to get reader feedback, pivot until you have the right book and build traction once you do.

© 2018 Stephen Gose

Also By Stephen Gose

Phaser3 Game Starter Kit Collection

Phaser Game Prototyping

Phaser Multi-player Gaming Systems

Phaser Game Starter Kit Collection

Kiwi Game Design Workbook

Phaser.js Game Design Workbook

Using JavaScript OLOO in game development

Making Dating & Quiz Games

Making Puzzle Browser Games with Phaser v2

Phaser v2 Game Design Workshop Course

Phaser III Game Design Workshop

Contents

I   Making Dress-Up Browser Games with Phaser 2   1

    Reference From: 1

    Overview 2

    Course Objectives: The Goal 3

1. **Lesson: Game Mechanics** 4

    Game Features 4

    Homework & Research: 5

2. **Lesson: Game Examples Research** 6

    Game Tools & Generators 7

    Exercise 2: 8

    Homework & Research: 8

3. **Lesson: Current Demand for Dress-UP Games** 9

    Homework & Research: 10

    Exercise 3: 10

4. **Lesson: Game Logic & Construction Considerations** 12

    Step #1 Find the avatar(s). 12

    Step #2 Create the wardrobe 15

    Step #3 Messy or tidy? 15

    Step #4 Layout Arrangement 16

    Step #5 Asset Download Considerations 17

CONTENTS

5. **Lesson 5: Game Flow** **19**

   Network Impact 21

II Starting the Dress-Up Game Project 25

   Step 0: Review these demonstrations: 27

6. **Step 1. Create our standard index file.** **28**

7. **Step 2. Create your standard game shell scenes.** **33**

   Dress-UP Core Game Phases 35

   Main.js 35

   Boot.js 39

   Preload.js 40

   Splash.js or Language.js 41

   Menu.js 43

   Play.js — Overview 45

   Dog.js – a gentle introduction to standard Dress-UP games 46

   Dog.js Create function – Lines 51 to 130 47

   Dog.js Create function – Lines 131 to 170 48

   Mark.js – adding clothes and toggles 49

   Miyoko.js – adding data structures and multiple spriteSheets management 49

   Managing Hair and "Split-ends" 49

   What's a Girl to Wear? Clothes management 50

   Zoe.js – the full Monty 50

8. **Common Menus** **52**

   Printing 54

   Saving 55

   Camera Snap-shots 58

9. **Conclusion** **61**

Copyright © 1972-2017, Stephen Gose. All rights reserved.

CONTENTS

More Game Starter Kit Tutorials 61
Further Information 61
Introduction References 62

Making Dress-Up Browser Games with Phaser 2

A Starter Kit Tutorial for Dress-Up & Fashions Game Mechanics

If you would like a *Course Completion Certificate*, please answer all the quiz questions at the end of each lesson.

- Use the *Menu to navigate* between topic in the course.
- If you would like a *Course Completion Certificate*, please answer all the quiz questions at the end of each lesson.
- You will have *two chances to pass each end-of-lesson quiz*.
- You have a *limited number of attempts to complete this course*.
- There is *no expiration date* for this course.

Reference From:

This tutorial is a single chapter from a larger collection of 16 game mechanics found on http://leanpub.com/pgskc/

- Supporting website and bonus content: http://makingbrowsergames.com/starterkits/dressup/
- Game Design Workbook - https://leanpub.com/phaserjsgamedesignworkbook;
- Phaser Game Prototypes - https://leanpub.com/LoRD;

- Phaser Game Development Library - https://leanpub.com/b/phasergamedevelopment,
- Ultimate Phaser Library - https://leanpub.com/b/ultimatephaserlibrary

This tutorial is an abridged edition; it links to 276 additional pages of content. We chose this format to reduce the retail price while still supplying value. *In all, this tutorial is 317+ pages of total content.*

Overview

Dress-Up games are the central pillar of online gaming! Have you ever created an avatar? Customized their armor? **You've played a dress-up game**. The Dress-UP Game Starter Kit is an easy-to-use blueprint for ***Phaser.js JavaScript Gaming Framework*** for either the official or Community Editions v2.x.x API; it has all the game mechanism and logic that you need for a complete *Dress-Up* game. Phaser is one of the best HTML5 / JavaScript game development frameworks on the Internet. It is certainly a powerful tool when combined with GUI-editors and Cocoon. Phaser liberates your design decisions since it is pure JavaScript. It gives complete freedom over your game design patterns, artwork selections, and your chosen deployment venues. I have been using Phaser Game Framework for quite some time now; and, have created this series of "Game Starter Kit & Blue Prints" which you might find beneficial in launching your own game projects. Furthermore, I created other game development tools to help me generate new game ideas.

Visit http://makingbrowsergames.com/gameDesigner/ **and try them yourself.**

You might wonder "why would anyone want to create such an online game?" Well, during my research for this chapter, I thought the same thing; **but, what I found is truly amazing.** Not only is "Dress-UP and Fashions" an ancient game mechanics, it also *boasts several patents and thousands of variations.*

Course Objectives: The Goal

I would like to guide you in creating **several styles of Dress-UP** games mechanics. We will use the game mechanics, mechanisms and the development methods discussed in *Phaser Game Prototypes.** By the end of this tutorial, you should have a fully functional **Dress-Up** game using your own gaming assets. Here is the website where you can download the bonus content included with your book purchase.

Visit http://makingbrowsergames.com/starterkits/ and try them yourself.

---
*http://leanpub.com/LoRD

1. Lesson: Game Mechanics

A Dress-UP (or sometimes called Fashions) game mechanics is a simple "drop-n-drag" or "click & point" designed for non-competitive children's entertainment. This game mechanic can be traced back to the earliest toys around 900 AD* and to the early 1700s as "paper dolls"†. In the 20th century, the fascination with fashion and paper dolls was dominated by the **creations**‡ of Tom Tierney§ published in books, newspapers, and magazines. More about the growth of this game genre and innovation toward *"Pink software"* successes are found here.¶

Generally, the game involves decorating a pet animal or avatar with clothing articles, jewelry, and cosmetics. The game's intent — since it is a form of make-believe and role-playing — is to develop and to help children with their imagination, fashion style, and color coordination. Wikipedia states it this way,

> More and more *tweens*‖ are taking to the internet to talk with friends, shop and play games. In recent years, the most popular girl's games have been dress up and fashion games which allow girls to dress and customize virtual dolls, go shopping and complete challenges. The newest virtual dress up sites allow users to make new friends and chat with other users while they play with their pretend dolls. ... The game is most popular among girls worldwide, usually from ages 2–8

Game Features

Dress-UP games typically have the following mechanisms and game mechanics:

---

* http://www.opdag.com/history.html
† https://en.wikipedia.org/wiki/Paper_doll
‡ Margalit Fox (July 18, 2014). "Tom Tierney, Who Made Paper Dolls an Art Form, Dies at 85". The New York Times. Retrieved 2014-08-17.
§ https://www.tomtierneystudios.com/
¶ https://killscreen.com/articles/awfulness-and-importance-dress-game/
‖ https://www.urbandictionary.com/define.php?term=tween

Lesson: Game Mechanics

- Cycling buttons dynamically based on sprite sheets and objects passed to the play state.
- Tilemap Creation of various clothing, jewelry, and cosmetics.
- Basic avatar selection.
- Recursive logic for Match validation and removal.
- Tile click/hit detection.
- "Drop and drag" and "snap-to-grid" capabilities.
- Arcade physics detection.
- Save and print final avatar display.
- Are intensive and requires bandwidth optimizations for artwork downloads.

Homework & Research:

- http://www.opdag.com/history.html
- https://www.tomtierneystudios.com/
- https://killscreen.com/articles/awfulness-and-importance-dress-game/

Take this quiz online*

*http://leanpub.com/courses/leanpub/mbg-dressup-p2/quizzes/lesson1-1

2. Lesson: Game Examples Research

Paraphrased from Wikipedia, "One of the most notable early adaptors of virtual dress-up technology was the **_Kisekae_** – meaning "to dress" in Japanese – System Sets (KiSS). The games featured a lingerie-clad doll figurine and a small, often suggestive, wardrobe; each item snaps into place once you dragged it on to the doll, and thus simulate "dressing" her. These stand-alone games initially featured a manga-styled model and a small wardrobe. Eric Zimmerman and Elena Gorfinkel pointed out that KiSS games are implicitly adult in nature, as "the open-ended play of paper dolls shifts into a game of interactive striptease." Frequently, the KiSS games were not about using clothing fashions creatively, but rather the sexually-alluring illustrated girl.

The next phenomenon was "Dollz"* — small, pixel-art `.gif` images which were presented scattered across websites, and allowed users to be dragged "into the pixel dolls."† Dollz Mania website‡, in my opinion, has mastered the concepts of Dress-UP game mechanics. They will become our mentor in dress-up fashions game and how to design the associated artwork.

---

*http://www.dollzmania.com/
†Mariam Naziripour (February 26, 2014). "The Awfulness and the Importance of the Dress-Up Game". Kill Screen. Retrieved 2014-08-17.
‡http://www.dollzmania.com/

Lesson: Game Examples Research

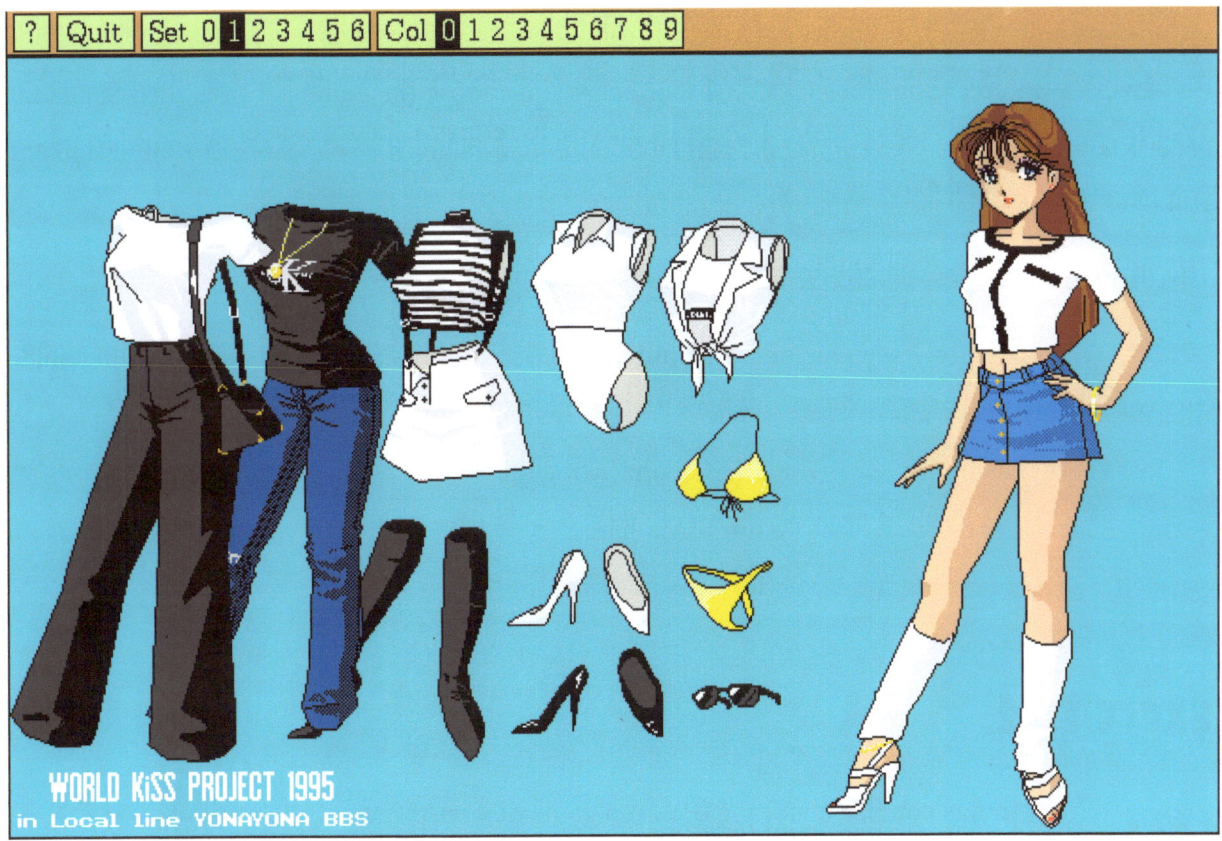

1995 KiSS Demonstration- see website animation

 see website animation: http://makingbrowsergames.com/starterkits/dressup/

Game Tools & Generators

You will discover many supporting tools from GitHub and the Appendix in this book. There are tools that will help in the generating gaming ideas.

Random Game Mechanics Generator* — This idea generation machine randomly selects 3 — by default — common game theory mechanics. The game mechanics and descriptions should help your imagination blend and produce the next blockbuster game.

*http://makingbrowsergames.com/gameDesigner/index-randommechanic.html

Game Mechanisms* — This library of game controls and mechanism spans several JavaScript gaming frameworks. (more are on the way!) This tool helps you choose the game controls then opens the generic code snapshots (aka snippets). Spend a minute to re-factor the snapshots to your design and you have a functional game prototype in minutes.

This Tutorial offers several unique demonstrations examples:

- Create Your Own Trix† — demo and transpiled from our 2011 released Flash ActionScript game.
- Game of Thrones by Doll Dive‡ — released Flash ActionScript game.
- Super Hero Creator§ — released Flash ActionScript game.
- Marvel Hero¶ — released Flash ActionScript game.
- http://www.dollzmania.com/ website. *(worth studying!)*

Exercise 2:

- Write down 3 things you like about the dress-up game demonstration.
- Write down 3 things you would change, add, or modify.

Homework & Research:

- http://www.opdag.com/history.html
- https://www.tomtierneystudios.com/
- https://killscreen.com/articles/awfulness-and-importance-dress-game/

Take this quiz online‖

---

* http://makingbrowsergames.com/gameDesigner/index-controlMechanisms.html
† http://makingbrowsergames.com/starterkits/dressup/avatarEditor-CS4f10as3-v0.html
‡ http://www.dolldivine.com/game-of-thrones.php
§ https://www.newgrounds.com/portal/view/657097
¶ http://www.marvelhq.com/create-your-own-super-hero
‖ http://leanpub.com/courses/leanpub/mbg-dressup-p2/quizzes/lesson2

3. Lesson: Current Demand for Dress-UP Games

Take a look at the Phaser forum and you should find a cry for more Fashion / Dress-UP games = We need girly dress up games.* This plea comes from Melodi (http://melodimedia.com/) a prominent leading specialist in mobile content solutions. Melodi provides a wealth of services to the mobile industry from content production, aggregation and distribution, through to fully fledged content management and white label / fully managed solutions.

On behalf of their clients, they run more than 1000+ fully managed mobile app stores targeting diverse audiences all over the planet. They provide services in **over 65 countries and in over 20 languages (!)** with particularly strong focus on the EMEA† and LATAM‡ regions, offering localized language content that is culturally relevant and targeted. Research their website here.§

---

*http://www.html5gamedevs.com/topic/8924-generate-income-from-html5-we-need-girly-dress-up-games/
†https://en.wikipedia.org/wiki/Europe,_the_Middle_East_and_Africa
‡https://en.wikipedia.org/wiki/Latin_America
§http://www.melodimedia.co.uk/about-melodi-media/

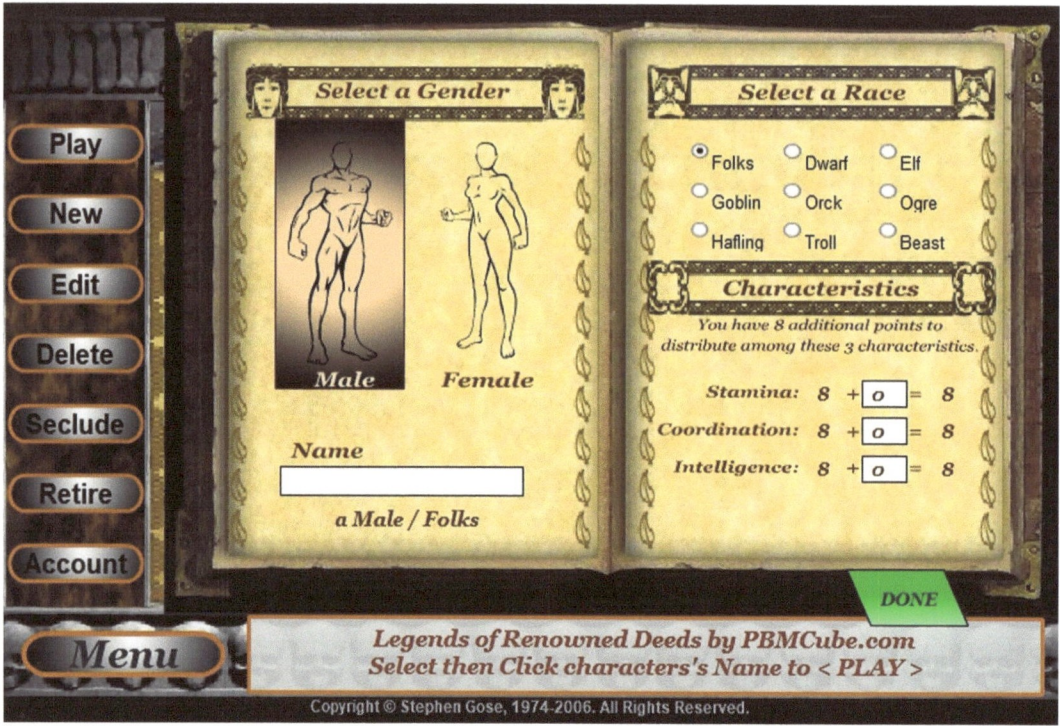

Dress-UP mechanics in Avatar Creations

Homework & Research:

- http://www.html5gamedevs.com/topic/8924-generate-income-from-html5-we-need-girly-dress-up-games/

- http://www.melodimedia.co.uk/about-melodi-media/

Exercise 3:

? Write down 3 ways Melodi could help distribute your finished game(s).

? Write down other services Melodi provides or offers.

? What is the process to license you game with Melodi?

? Research tween preferences for EMEA* and LATAM† regions.

Take this quiz online‡

---
*https://en.wikipedia.org/wiki/Europe,_the_Middle_East_and_Africa
†https://en.wikipedia.org/wiki/Latin_America
‡http://leanpub.com/courses/leanpub/mbg-dressup-p2/quizzes/lesson3

4. Lesson: Game Logic & Construction Considerations

At first glance, a dress-up fashion game seems simple enough. You simply add some clothes, jewelry, make-up, a choice of avatar bodies and features, and deploy to the masses. Let's take a step back and consider a few pointers.

- What avatars and what poses to use.
- How many articles are in a wardrobe? Where could you find them? Who will draw them?
- Do socks go inside or outside the shoes?
- Do folks wear their "underwear" outside or inside their clothing?
- Does hair-styles go in front or in back of the head?
- Does hair drape in front or behind the shoulders?
- Will the avatar have layers of clothing such as a coat or cape?

From these few questions, we have learned that layers and positioning for various clothing becomes important. The game will require a lot of tailored artwork. The wardrobe items must match the avatar's body; if gamers have a choice of avatars then all clothing articles must match all avatars. Scale and precision placement on the avatar(s) are crucial. If "point & click" is used, instead of "drag & drop", then avatar's stage position is also crucial.

Discouraged? Ah! let's just eat this elephant one byte at a time! ... eat faster! Let's research the answers since building a *Dress-UP* takes an "inside out" development process.

Step #1 Find the avatar(s):

Dreamstime has royalty-free stock silhouettes*. You can download images for *FREE after registra-*

---
*https://www.dreamstime.com/#res20585143

Lesson: Game Logic & Construction Considerations

tion.* If we permit different body shapes as illustrated below, we must switch wardrobe articles to fit either the slim or voluptuous.

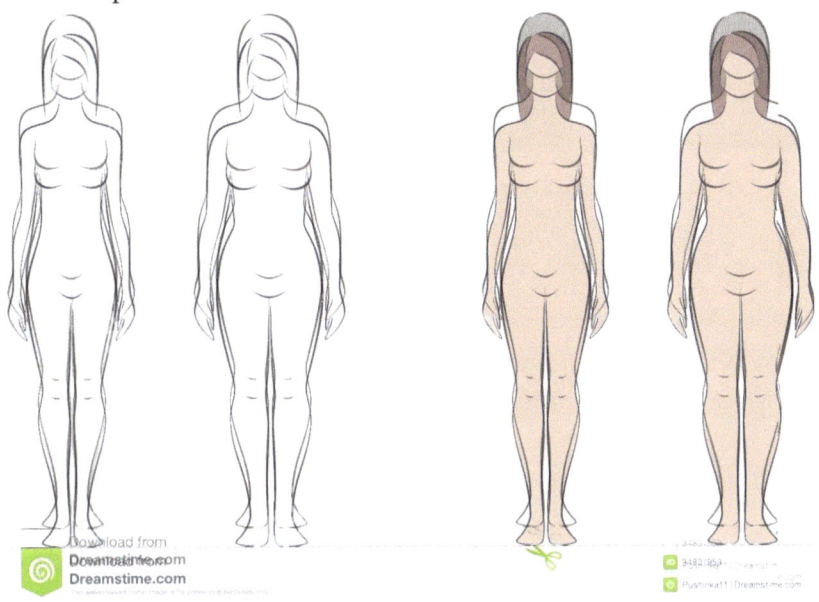

Search of Line Drawn Silhouettes

We will use the line drawing silhouettes and allow our gamers to choose the ethnic flavors. We can change the tint on the manikin.

---

* https://www.dreamstime.com/register#res20585143

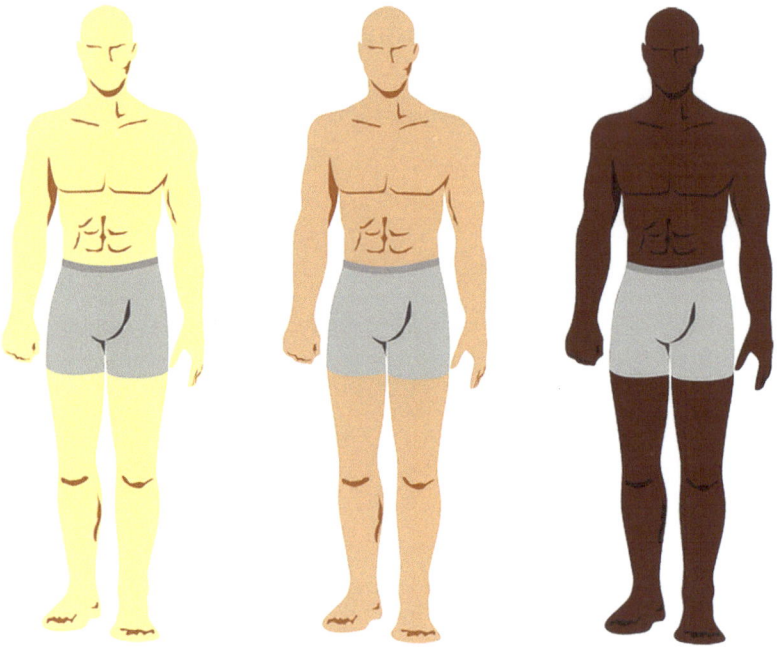

Using tint to create ethnic flavors

Another consideration is the gender and age. Will we offer male, female and children manikin? This decision will increase the clothing articles in the wardrobe.

A final consideration is the manikin's position and posture.

Avatar posture sets the mood.

Step #2 Create the wardrobe

Finding random fashion items from the Internet is wonderful, but the clothing must fit the body of the manikin. Each clothing article should be drawn to scale on top of the body to ensure its proper fitting.

Each item could be a separate sprite in a "drag and drop" fashion game. This means that each item will need `Arcade Physic` and `listeners` to respond to the mouse clicks. I prefer to use "previous" and "next" buttons because this allows switch clothing within a spriteSheet from one frame to the next. This also provides accurate placement and avoids "what on top of what" problems.

Step #3 Messy or tidy?

Where do you want all those clothes? Strewn about the game board? Or nicely hung in a closet? Remember, this is a childrens' (?) game; what are we subtly teaching them about care and maintenance of their possessions?

Step #4 Layout Arrangement

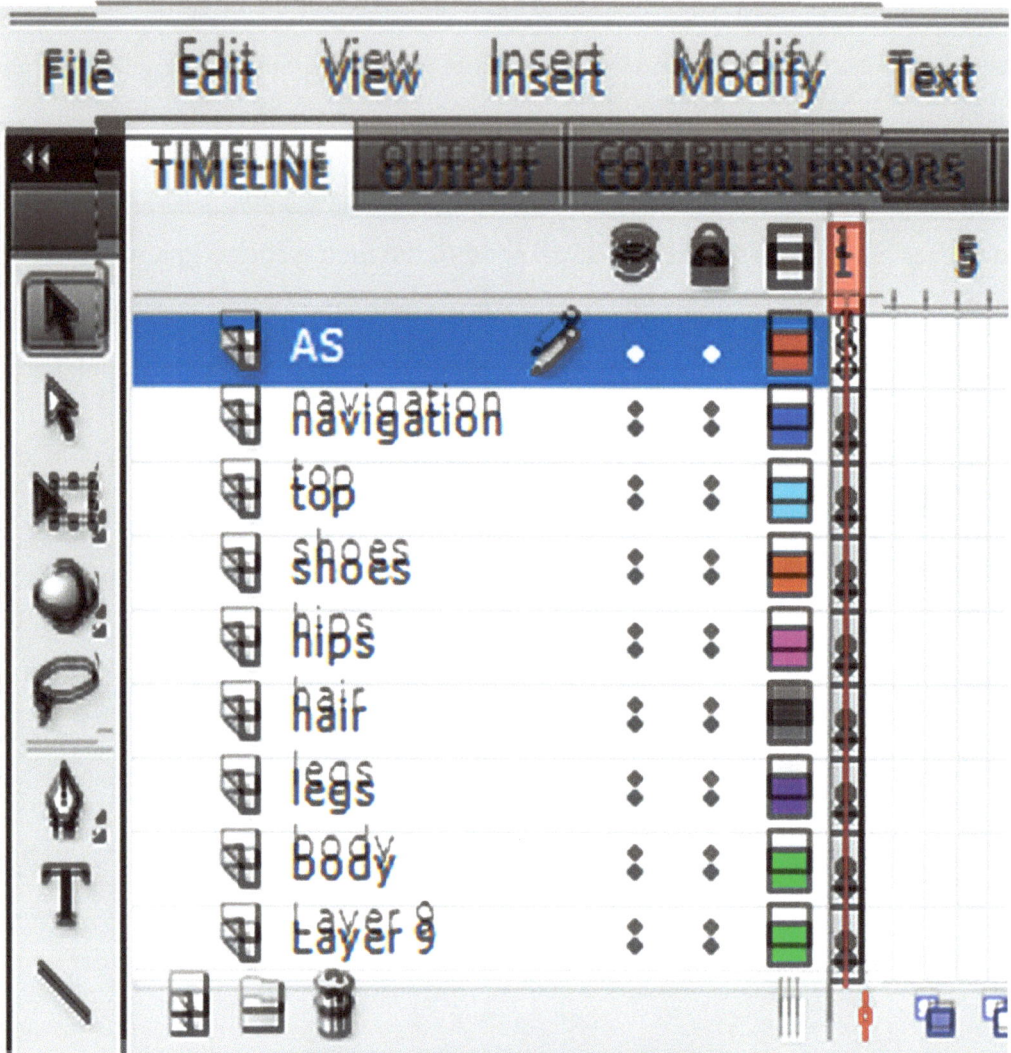

Image layers and placement are critical

The avatar is stacked above any background layer or themes. The facial features and then any cosmetics would be the next layers above the body, if you provide those options. The next layer is the clothing for the legs such as socks, pants, etc.

 Remember, the order of the layers and which one is on top is important.

Lesson: Game Logic & Construction Considerations

Hairstyles are tricky because the hair falls in back of the face but in front of the eyebrows and over the top of body's shoulders. Sections of the hair may cover portions of the face (such as "bangs" and the correct style for face shape. Hairstyles are groups; the parts placed on top of the face, the parts that fall behind the head and the parts that fall on top of the shoulders.

Problematic Hair or Bad hair day placement

 The secret sauce that makes everything align properly is the sprite.anchor orientation. Refer to https://phaser.io/examples/v2/sprites/anchor

Step #5 Asset Download Considerations

Downloading Dress-UP game assets are split up into two considerations depending on how often each is used in the game and across the game phases.

"GLOBAL" assets are loaded from the start of the game during the boot, pre-load and main menu phases. These assets are typically used in multiple game phases. The one exception to this is the splash and/or main-menu theme or background graphics.

All *"OTHER"* assets are loaded when the game enters their respective game levels. In this case, it is when the game switches to a selected character from the main menu. You can tell these assets are loading when a 'spinner' is displayed.

5. Lesson 5: Game Flow

When a gamer launches our featured game from the `index.html` page, we lead them through a series of menu screens or game phases. Eventually, they will click a "play" button somewhere on the "main menu" to start the "Game Loop". Download the Game Flowchart from

http://makingbrowsergames.com/starterkits/_GameFlowChart.pdf

Each screen has "its own internal essential functions". These phases give a way to organize our code into modules and ensure that only the minimal game assets (for this current phase) are supplied at just the proper time. These "game scene modules" help us isolate distinct phases from each other. For example, booting the game; loading assets; main menu; playing level one, two, winning, losing, etc. This is an important concept in the new Phaser v3 since game scenes in Phaser v3 are more autonomous. The goal we achieve, by using this "finite state machine" structure, makes our game development simpler and less painful to support.

Lesson 5: Game Flow

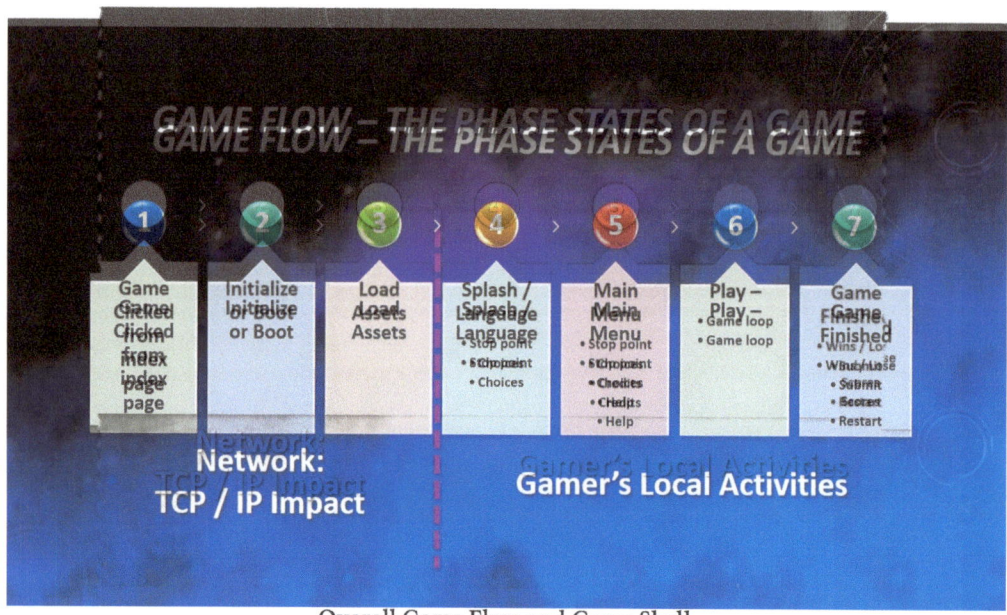

Overall Game Flow and Game Shell

Each of those phases is governed internally by the "Essential" Phaser functions (listed below). Each Game Screen's responsibility is to control the flow of each game flow phases. Each of these "Essential Phaser Functions" is included in every scene.

- The "Initiate or Boot" phase sets-up current variables, canvas dimensions, browser orientation, and data for this specific scene.
- The "preload" phase manages the game assets, downloading, and storing them in each unique Phaser Cache. This is an extremely important phase for Dress-Up games since the volume of artwork to download is quite extensive. To optimize, create spriteSheets.
- The "create" phase makes the loaded game assets available.
- The "update" phase attempts to collect the "whereabouts" of all the game assets on the stage (aka camera view) at approximately 60 frames per second (fps). In Phaser v3, you now have the option to manage the fps using the Tween Manager.
- The "render" phase publishes the new game asset positions. In Phaser v3, you now have a choice of "Dynamic" or "Static" rendering.

Network Impact

Let's review the first three typical states after the `index.html` page: boot, preload, and splash scenes. In practice, your gamers would see a progress bar then after a few seconds, the first "splash" or "language selection" menu. The network has the most impact on our game during these initial phases.

Placing our game as close to the player will help their perception of how quick and lively our game is. "How do we ensure our game deployment is close to our consumers?", you say. By using a content delivery network! The sample `index.html` source code offers two choices to pull the Phaser framework from a content delivery network. Once your game reaches the "splash/language" scene, all activity is on the gamers' device as a "single-player" game. You'll find the following phrase, "Stop point" in illustration below. What I mean is these are excellent times to load additional game assets. Your game has met the "App Stores" requirements on activation within 20 seconds; now, while the gamer is considering various choices you offered, is the perfect time to turn on web sockets or download further assets in the background.

Each of those phases is governed internally by the "Essential" Phaser functions (listed below). Each Game Screen's responsibility is to control the flow of each game flow phases. Each of these "Essential Phaser Functions" is included in every scene.

- The "Initiate or Boot": http://makingbrowsergames.com/starterkits/dressup/v2_dressup_bootJS.pdf phase sets-up current variables, canvas dimensions, browser orientation, and data for this specific scene.
- The "preload" phase manages the game assets, downloading, and storing them in each unique Phaser Cache.
- The "create" phase makes the loaded game assets available.
- The "update" phase attempts to collect the "whereabouts" of all the game assets on the stage (aka camera view) at approximately 60 frames per second (fps). In Phaser v3, you now have the option to manage the fps using the Tween Manager.

Lesson 5: Game Flow

- The "render" phase publishes the new game asset positions. In Phaser v3, you now have a choice of "Dynamic" or "Static" rendering.

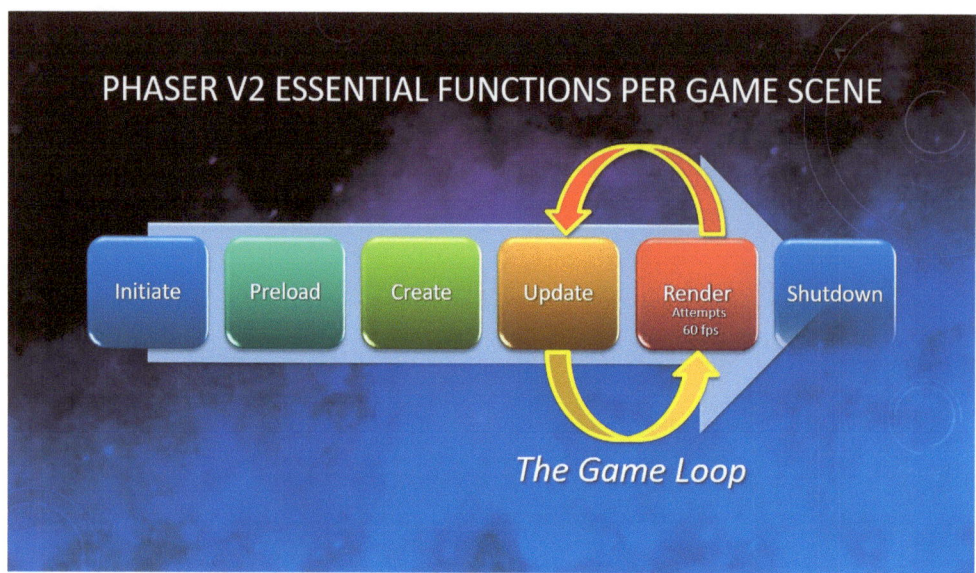

Figure: Phaser Essential Functions

The Game loop's responsibility, illustrated above, is to control the flow of several game elements. The Game Loop is the standard "universal process" of **input, process, and output**. It re-cycles until the game migrates to a new phase. The Phaser v2 game loop has many moving parts inside, and the render phase attempts to maintain a rate of 60 times per second.

Lesson 5: Game Flow

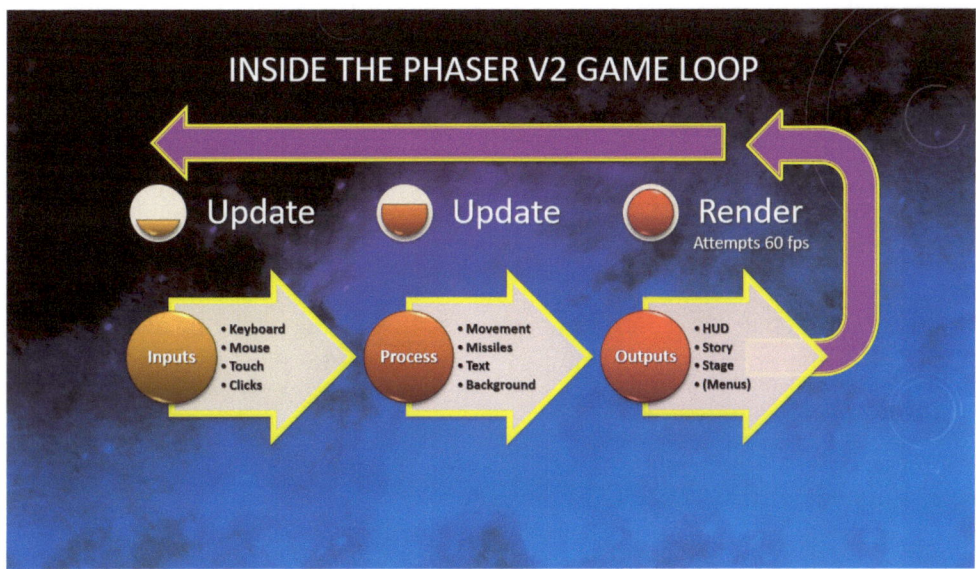

Figure: Phaser v2 Game Loop

Let's write some more code. Here's what our *Phaser v2 game skeleton framework* looks like. The following code is generic style across all Phaser v2 games; it is called "game.js" (or "main.js"). This will be our standard game creation template **for Phaser v2** called "game Skeleton". Phaser 3 is extremely flexible and adds several innovative ways to achieve this similar "game set-up".

Our game is a simple JavaScript Object resting inside the Browser Object Model (BOM) "window".[^27] W3Schools states, "The Browser Object Model (BOM) allows JavaScript to "talk to" the browser. ... There are no official standards for the **B**rowser **O**bject **M**odel (BOM). ... The **window** object is supported by all browsers. It represents the browser's window. All global JavaScript objects, functions, and variables automatically become members of the window object."[^28]

Note: This example is available as a bonus content download from http://makingbrowsergames.com/starterkits/_v2gameSkeletonJS.pdf

- Reference 1, we "use strict"[^29] to avoid fat-fingering, nasty bugs, poor assignments and the like. Comments are our friend. Use them generously! Console logging is our best friend and worth the investigation to use properly.[^30]

- Reference 2: Let's declare the global application object or "namespace". This creates our JavaScript game (object) = the "constructor", and inside we set the game's dimensions to the Golden ratio.[^31] Our Phaser game will live inside this JavaScript object and is protected from memory collisions; this is a "namespace technique".[^32] Also, our game states (the various phases and menus a gamer would migrate through to play our game) will be kept safely in this global object.[^33] This article is an excellent primer for the new Phaser v3 namespaces and game scenes.[^34] The suggests here are not the only way to create JavaScript namespaces; this is one of the hardest concepts for those new to the Phaser Game Framework. Trying to understand why Phaser games look so different is best explained by this side-trip article.[^35]

- Reference 3: extends our newly created "Game" object with a prototype inheritance chain. This attaches all our internal game functions to our newly created object above.
- Reference 4: our preload game assets. Remember the game must be active within 20 seconds or we stand rejection from the "app stores".
- Reference 5: create links our newly downloaded assets into the game.
- Reference 6: update will continually read the inputs and modifications and render the results to the gamer.
- Reference 7: render is reserved for new information after the displayed updates and debug information.
- Reference 8: Ties the Phaser Game Engine and framework into a variable for our DOM canvas tag.
- Reference 9: are a glimpse into what's new in the upcoming Phaser v3 – to quote Dorothy from the Wizard of Oz, "We're not in Kansas anymore!"

11 Starting the Dress-Up Game Project

At a minimum, we need two files and two directory folders:

1. An index.html file that launches our game,
2. A game.js file — name it anything you'd like — place it inside a newly created JavaScript ("js") directory folder; and finally
3. An assets directory folder in which we'll store all our game graphics, sounds, and images.

```
 1     :(top root directory - single player)
 2     ├── favicon.ico
 3     ├── index.html
 4     ├── license.txt
 5     ├── manifest.json
 6     ├── package.json            //for Progressive Web Applications
 7     ├── PurchaseOrder.pdf
 8     ├── ReadMe.md
 9     |
10     ├── assets
11     |   ├── audio
12     |   ├── images
13     |   └── spriteSheets
14     |
15     ├── css
16     |   └── main.css
17     ├── fonts
18     |   └── fonts.css
```

```
19        │
20        └── js
21              ├── libraries
22              ├── plugins
23              ├── prefabs
24              ├── states
25              └── utilities
```

I label "assets" as the place to hold all game images, sprites, and sounds — since I am the original creator of them, and they are copyrightable[1]. Let's not worry about putting any of these items in the "asset directory folders" for now. We'll do that later – after we have our source code drafted and operational. Here's what another famous game developer says:

> "Challenge yourself to create a code-base that compiles and runs in the first few hours. Make it so that you can accept inputs, move around, animate something, and trigger some sounds. This prototype, lousy a game as it may be, is going to be your best friend. The sooner you can have a working early playable prototype, the more likely you are to succeed.
>
> No-art prototypes also have one other major advantage: in previous games, I would make beautiful mock-ups in PhotoShop and gather hundreds of lovely looking sprites in preparation for the game. After development was complete, the vast majority of the art had to be replaced, re-sized, or thrown out. I've wasted thousands of hours making game-ready artwork before coding; these days I know that the tech specs and evolving game-play mechanics will mean that much of what you make at the start won't make it into the finished game." by Christer Kaitila: The Chunky-pants Method

 Tip: These are part of the Bonus Content downloads at http://makingbrowsergames.com/starterkits/dressup/ You can review more game mechanics at our supporting website — http://makingbrowsergames.com/starterkits/

These are the general exercise steps we will follow as we build our game project:

Step 0. Preparation. This is the fun part of development; so, have a party and enjoy!

- **Research and play similar gaming ideas currently on the market.**

- **Write your ideas down or use the** Game Generation Tools above

- **Build your Workstation and File Structure.**

Step 1. Create your game's index file. Always use "responsive design" and determine whether you want a "Standard", "Single Web Page Application"[*] or Progressive Web App (PWA)[†] deployment.

Step 2. Create your game shell scenes as "Standalone" or Content Management System (CMS).

Step 3. Create your game core functions and `play` scene.

Step 0: Review these demonstrations:

- http://makingbrowsergames.com/starterkits/dressup/

- Trix Attacks Magix - Create Your Own Trix[‡]

- Zoe Dress-UP[§]

- Other examples are on this course's website[¶] ...

Notes

[1] Now might be a good time to review what the US Copyrights & Patent Office says concerning games and copyrights. Read: https://www.copyright.gov/fls/fl108.pdf

---

[*] https://www.seguetech.com/what-is-a-single-page-application/
[†] https://developers.google.com/web/progressive-web-apps/
[‡] http://makingbrowsergames.com/starterkits/dressup/avatarEditor-CS4f10as3-v0.html
[§] http://makingbrowsergames.com/starterkits/dressup/v2.6.2/index.html
[¶] http://makingbrowsergames.com/starterkits/dressup/

6. Step 1: Create our standard index file.

Let's create two distinctive "front-door delivery systems" for our games. The first delivery version is through a standard index.html web page, and the second version is tailored for mobile devices as a "single web page application" (SWPA)* or Progressive Web App (PWA).† I recommend using a "mobile first, responsive design" HTML page for all.

We'll begin working on our game's "standard front door" — the index.html file. Create or download it. This file must be labeled "**index.html**"; this is, unfortunately, NOT a choice in our game development.

 If you're curious as to why? I recommend a side-trip to this article on "Why is it important that we name the main file index.html?"‡

---

*https://en.wikipedia.org/wiki/Single-page_application
†https://developers.google.com/web/progressive-web-apps/
‡https://teamtreehouse.com/community/why-is-it-important-that-we-name-the-main-file-indexhtml

Step 1: Create our standard index file.

Standard HTML5 Index page

```html
<!doctype html>
<html lang="en">
<head>
    <meta charset="UTF-8" />
    <title>Phaser Game Prototyping - (Your Game Title Here) </title>
    <meta name="description" content="Phaser Game Prototyping Template" />
    <link rel="shortcut icon" href="favicon.ico" type="image/x-icon" />
    <style>
        body {margin:0; padding:0; background: #000;}
        canvas {margin: 0 auto;}
    </style>
    <link rel="stylesheet" type="text/css" href="fonts/fonts.css" />
    <link rel="stylesheet" type="text/css" href="css/main.css" />
    <link rel="icon" href="assets/launcher.png" type="image/png" />
    <!-- Required for Progressive Web Application -->
    <link rel="manifest" href="manifest.json" />
    <!--
    <script src="https://cdnjs.cloudflare.com/ajax/libs/ phaser-ce/ 2.10.6 / phaser.min.js">  </script>
    OR
    <script src="js/phaser3.10.4.min.js"></script>
    -->
    <script src="https://cdn.jsdelivr.net/phaser/2.6.2/phaser.min.js"></script>
    <script defer src="js/main.js"></script>

    <script defer src="js/state/boot.js"></script>
    <script defer src="js/state/credits.js"></script>
    <script defer src="js/state/demo.js"></script>
    <script defer src="js/state/load.js"></script>
    <script defer src="js/state/menu.js"></script>
    <script defer src="js/state/play.js"></script>

</head>
<body itemscope itemtype="http://schema.org/CreativeWork/WebApplication">
    <div id="orientation"></div>
    <!--
    NOTE: Phaser library must be loaded prior to any game logic.
    We load script files here to avoid window.onload call.
    Window.onload is rarely used for many reasons, and because
        Phaser doesn't wait until all resources are loaded.
    The DOMContentLoaded event triggers when the page is ready.
```

Step 1. Create our standard index file. 30

```
43           It waits for the full HTML and scripts and then starts.
44           This is explained in greater detail in
45                "Phaser.JS Design Guide workbook".
46           NOTE: per the Phaser.JS Design Guide workbook, you may place the following
47           script externally or as the last head script using defer.
48           -->
49
50      </body>
51 </html>
```

I prefer loading the game directly into the document.body. Other game developers load their games into a parent <div> tag as a container. It's your choice. Which is best? Take a side-trip to this answer from Adobe . W3Schools.com provides this warning concerning <div> tags saying, "Note: By default, browsers always place a line break before and after the <div> element. However, this can be changed with CSS."

Did you notice how many JavaScript files we're using for our game? During development, this is "ok" and gives you the chance to quickly find those pesky software bugs. The downside is the added time to download and execute each JavaScript file. That's the reason I use "defer" inside the script tags. To compensate for the individual downloads, many developers will use Browserify to create one huge, monolithic, compressed file.

Notice you do not need to change any of its content! This is because we created this initial "front door into our game" in a standard generic format that applies to any game creation within this series. Software engineers call this ***D.R.Y. (Don't Repeat Yourself)*** coding; it saves your time by creating things once and re-using them; it's a *"building block style" or black-box development.* I said this before, *"Imagine within one year from now, you could have 12 to 52 games in the "Apps Stores"; the secret is keeping your code D.R.Y!*

 This example is available as a bonus content download from http://makingbrowsergames.com/starterkits/_indexHTML5.pdf.

Step 1. Create our standard index file. 31

Mobile Single Web Page Applications

Now for the tailored mobile device index page. This construction is different than before; my goal is to load as much as possible into the single page without exceeding 20 seconds. I have two different styles of pages for mobile devices. The example below creates a normal JavaScript link to the main.js (or game.js). I take a "less formal" approach in the mobile versions and try to "in-line" scripts inside the `index.html`'s `<div>` tags. The single web page application is divided into `<div>` sections. Each `<div>` section represents a single scene and the `game.js` is placed into the "play game" `<div>`. If the game is small, I will simply insert the entire raw `game.js` contents directly into a script tag and thus avoid an additional file to download. Do so, ensures the game content is a part of the `index.html` page.

Single Web Page Application

```
1       <!doctype html>
2       <html lang="en">
3       <head> . . . . .
4       </head>
5       <body> . . . .
6
7  <!-- Mobile Dress-UP game -->
8  <div  class="ui-content" data-theme="b" data-role="page" id="game">
9          <div data-role="header">
10             <h1><b>(Your Game Title here)</b></h1>
11         <a href=" " class="ui-btn ui-mini ui-icon-home ui-btn-icon-left ">Home</a>
12         </div>
13
14         <div id="game-area" data-role="main" class="ui-content">
15         </div>
16
17         <script src="game.js"></script>
18
19         <div class="ui-content center footer" data-role="footer">
20         <hr class="center" style="width: 60%" />
21         <nav class="menu"><a href='http://www.copyright.gov/fls/fl108.pdf' target='_blank'>\
22  Copyright </a> &copy; 1978-2016, <a class="w3-btn btn-footer w3-hover-deep-orange w\
23  3-theme-d3 w3-round-xlarge w3-border w3-text-shadow " href='http://www.stephen-gose.\
24  com/en/' target='_blank'> Stephen Gose LLC </a>. <br />All Rights Reserved. <br />Qu\
25  estions or comments? <a class="w3-btn btn-footer w3-hover-deep-orange w3-theme-d3 w3\
```

Step 1: Create our standard index file.

```
26       =round-xlarge w3-border w3-text-shadow " href="http://www.stephen-gose.com/about/con\
27       tact/"> Please Contact </a><br />
28             <hr class="center" style="width: 60%" />
29          </nav>
30       </div>
31    </div>
32    <!-- End Game Page -->
```

You can review it as a "single web page application" at:

http://makingbrowsergames.com/starterkits/dressup/v2.6.2-mobile/index.html

Sometimes, I like everything in one place; it depends on the size of the game I plan to deploy. All that remains is a method to bind all these into a single web page application (SWPA)[*]. Using a single monolithic file has advantages per Google's new(?) Accelerated Mobile Pages Project (AMP)[‡]. We'll do this through our game's index.html page. Many authors create yet another script file, but I prefer to use an inline scripting for mobile devices.

Excellent work! Our game page is ready to use and boot-up our game. Creating our game mechanics source code is our next "step"; let's move on to Step 2.

---
[*]https://www.seguetech.com/what-is-a-single-page-application/
[‡]https://www.ampproject.org/

7. Step 2: Create your standard game shell scenes.

Return to the Introduction section and review the Game Phases.

Choose whether we are creating a standard or mobile game. Then if you chose a mobile game, you should determine whether you want *a mobile "single web page application"* (SWPA) or a more traditional structure. The *single web page application* contains everything inside its `index.html` page. The `game.js` becomes a script tag inside one of the `<div>` tags as we discussed earlier. This will determine where the Main.js will reside. The earlier examples all used a "mobile first" responsive design in the `index.html`.

Let's create all the supporting game phases as separate JavaScript files. They all follow the generic format found in the Introduction Section: Phaser v2 Game Flow We'll place these files inside the `/js/states/` directory. Only a few changes are needed in the following files for this game genre:

- `Main.js` — which holds all the configuration characteristics and supporting functions of our games.
- `Boot.js` — designates our game assets to download. If we maintain the "naming convention", we simply have to create new artwork with the same file names found in the `boot.js` file and add any new items.
- `MainMenu.js` — perhaps small tweaks to our for unique options for this specific game?
- `Play.js` — which would normally be our game's loop; however, we will combine the play scene into the `mainMenu` scene. It will make perfect sense if you study the example on http://makingbrowsergames.com/starterkits/dressup/v2.6.2/index.html

 Press "F12" to watch the "behind the scenes" activities.

Step 2. Create your standard game shell scenes.

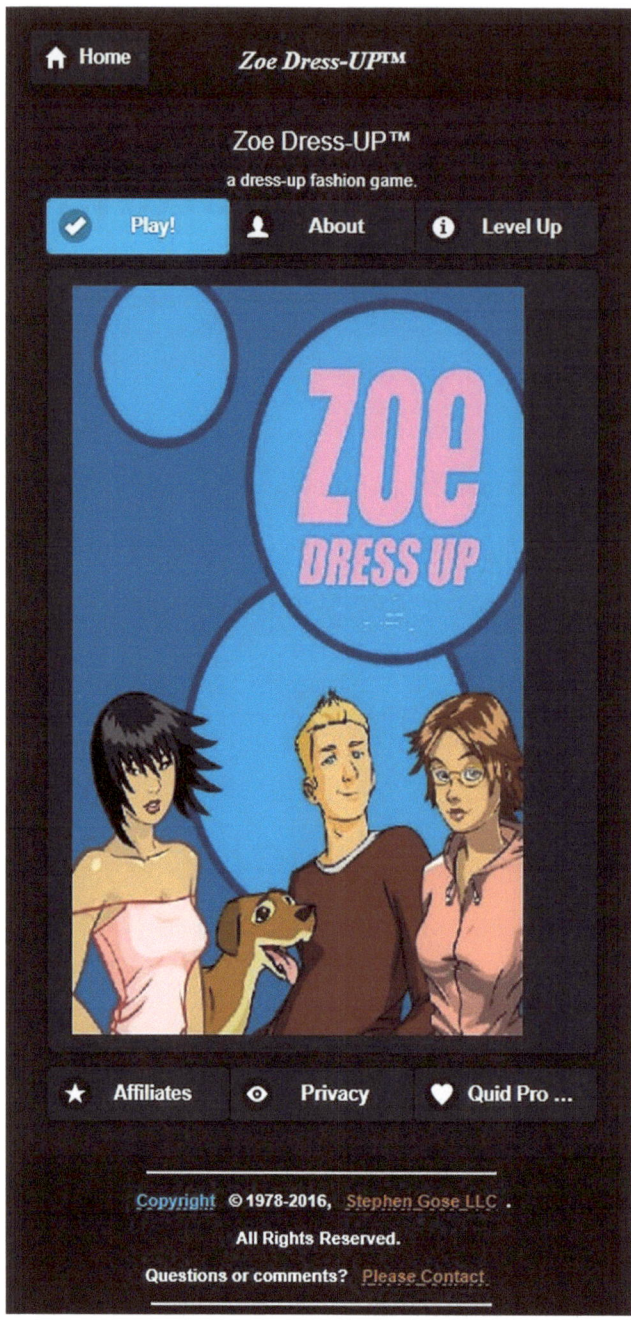

Mobile version with theme

Step 2. Create your standard game shell scenes.

Dress-UP Core Game Phases

We will create two distinctive delivery styles of Dress-UP games; one for normal web browser and the following tailored for a mobile device.

Main.js

This JavaScript file "IS" the game. It holds all the configuration logic used during the `play phase`. What you entitle this file is not critical, but always name it the same across all your projects. Why? Because we have a "D.R.Y." thing going on and we want "stay dry" — to keep our consistency across all our development projects. There's another reason: NAMESPACE SECURITY! As players launch and play our collection of games, one game will "over-write" another.

This file also holds our initial language text to prompt the player's selection. We use their selection to trigger a JSON language file.

>   *http://makingbrowsergames.com/starterkits/dressup/index.html*
>
>   http://makingbrowsergames.com/starterkits/dressup/v2_dressup_mainJS.pdf

```
 1   /**
 2    * File Name: Main.js (Dress-Up)
 3    * Live Demo: http://makingbrowsergames.com/starterkits/dressup/
 4    * Source Code: http://makingbrowsergames.com/starterkits/
 5    * Description: File for controlling and displaying game scenes;
 6    *     managing global variables throughout game state.
 7    * Author: Stephen Gose
 8    * Version: 0.0.0.17
 9    * Author URL: http://www.stephen-gose.com/
10    * Support: support@pbmcube.com
11    *
12    * Copyright © \u00A9 1974-2017 Stephen Gose LLC. All rights reserved.
13    *
14    * Do not sell! Do not distribute!
15    * This is a licensed permission file. Please refer to Terms of Use
```

Step 2: Create your standard game shell scenes.

```javascript
16          *       and End Users License Agreement (EULA).
17          *       Search for [ //**TODO** ] to tailor this file for your own use; doing so will void any support agreement.
18          *
19          *
20          *       Redistribution of part or whole of this file and the accompanying files is strictly prohibited.
21          *
22          *
23          */
24          /**            game set-up            **/
25          console.log ("%c       Starting my awesome MMoG game Prototype!       \n       Phaser Dress-UP Starter Kit  \n        Copyright \u00A9 1974-2017,  Stephen Gose.          \n    | http://shop.pbmcube.net/ |                     \n    | \u2665\u2665\u2665\u2665\u2665 -> $120 License included in book!        \n | Book available at: http://leanpub.com/LoRD |    ",
30                  "color:white; background:blue");
31
32          window.GAMEAPP = {
33              // reference to the Phaser.Game instance
34              game: null,
35              //US Copr. or Copyright
36              Copr: "Copyright © 2007-2017, Stephen Gose. All rights reserved.\n";
37
38              //Canvas dimensions: world and viewportHeight
39              //**TODO** adjust for your game deployment
40
41              //Canvas dimensions: world and viewports' Height and Width
42              //**TODO** adjust for your game deployment
43              viewportWidth: 1024,
44              viewportHeight: 640,                   //game view using Golden Ration
45              worldWidth: 1024,                      //world view using Golden Ration
46              worldHeight: 640,
47
48              // =======================================================
49              //**TODO** refactor and adjust for your game deployment
50              //      Trash Global Variables (alphabetical)
51              //      Here we have some global level vars that persist
52              regardless of State.
53              // =======================================================
54
55              gameLanguage: 0,                  //Default is English (American)
56              InfoText: "Default Language: English\n Select language then
57              \n click arrow to enter.",
58              introPara: "Zoe is meeting her friends at the park. \n
```

Step 2: Create your standard game shell scenes.

```javascript
                    Help her find the best fashions to wear...\n";

            //button styling
            styleBTN: {font: "26px Arial", fill: "#000000", align: "center"},
            // HUD styling
            //        hero text
            styleCmbtH: {font: "9px Arial", fill:"#66ffff", align: "center"},
            styleNarrH: {font: "9px Arial", fill: "#66ffff", align: "left" },
            //        monster text
            styleCmbtM: {font: "9px Arial", fill:"#66ff66", align: "center"},
            styleNarrM: {font: "9px Arial", fill: "#66ff66", align: "left" },
            //HUD styling
            styleHUD: {font: "14px Arial", fill: "#ff9900", align: "center"},
            //Room Alert styling
            styleRAsm: {font: "18px Arial", fill: "#ff9900", align: "center",
                wordWrap: true, wordWrapWidth: 430},
            //Room Alert styling
            styleRAsmDrk: {font: "18px Arial", fill: "#000", align: "center",
                wordWrap: true, wordWrapWidth: 430},
            //Room Alert Dark styling
            styleRA: {font: "28px Arial", fill: "#ff9900", align: "center" },
            //Room Alert Dark styling
            styleRADrk: {font: "28px Arial", fill: "#000", align: "center" },
            //Dynamic Story style
            styleStory: {font: "16px Arial", fill: "#ff9900", align: "left"},
            //toolTip styling
            styleTT: {font: "11px Arial", fill: "#ff9900", align: "center" },

            // here we will store all game phase/states
            //   state object filled as js files load.
            state: {},


// ============================================================
// --------------------------------------------
// Main game Handler methods
// --------------------------------------------
//**TODO**:
//         refactor and adjust for your game deployment
//         remove console debug information on public deployment
// ============================================================
            // main function
            main: function(){
```

Step 2. Create your standard game shell scenes.

```
102                         this.game = new Phaser.Game(
103                                 this.viewportWidth,
104                                 this.viewportHeight,
105                                 Phaser.AUTO,
106                                 document.body,
107                                 window.GAMEAPP.state.boot);
108                 },
109
110         // ===========================================================
111         // -------------------------------------------------
112         // Supporting game Function & Classes
113         // -------------------------------------------------
114         //**TODO**:
115         //      Change namespace from generic GAMEAPP to your project
116         //      refactor and adjust for your game deployment
117         //      remove console debug information on public deployment
118         // ===========================================================
119         //
120         // ===========================================================
121         _assignLanguage: function(){
122         //This could be loaded externally from a JSON file
123         //I choose to have this internal to avoid additional downloads.
124         // If loading a file from outside of the domain in which
125             the game is running
126         // a 'Access-Control-Allow-Origin' header must be
127             present on the server.
128             switch(GAMEAPP.gameLanguage){
129                 case 0:         //"english":
130                 console.log("English selected");
131                 GAMEAPP.credittxt= "Credits & Info";
132                 GAMEAPP.donatxt= "Support Us";
133                 GAMEAPP.helptxt= "Help & Instructions";
134                 GAMEAPP.introPara= "Zoe will meet her friends at the park.
135                         Help her find the best fashions to wear.\n";
136                 GAMEAPP.moretxt= "More games";
137                 GAMEAPP.opttxt= "Options";
138                 GAMEAPP.playtxt= "Start Game";
139                 GAMEAPP.sharetxt= "Share with friends";
140                 GAMEAPP.webtxt= "Webmaster License Info";
141                 break;
142
143         (etc. . . . . Review the download file for other languages)
144                 },
```

Step 2. Create your standard game shell scenes.

```
145         //
146         //
147         // ============================================================
148         // --------------------------------------------
149         // End Main game Handler
150         // --------------------------------------------
151         // ============================================================
152         /** DEPRECATED METHOD - NEVER EVER USE THIS AGAIN!
153          *       See Phaser.js Game Design Workbook for complete explanation
154          *       http://leanpub.com/phaserjsgamedesignworkbook
155          *       window.onload = function () {
156          *           let game = new Phaser.Game(0, 0, Phaser.AUTO, document.body);
157          *       };
158          */
159
160         //preferred launch method for BOM.
161         window.addEventListener('DOMContentLoaded', function(){
162                 window.GAMEAPP.main();
163         }, false);
164
165         /* End of file */
166         /* Location: ./js/main.js */
```

Boot.js

Our boot state was launched from our game's index.html page. This game phase has the responsibility of configuring and setting-up the HTML5 canvas, and game physics. As its name suggests, its purpose prepares the web browser and sets the game dimensions — loading various game assets and storing them in Phaser v2 cache, having them readily available when needed throughout the game. Once the canvas is prepared, it will typically hand-off control toward the next phase called the "load" phase.

Modification to this file should be minimal as long as you follow *a standard naming convention across all your games.* Loading the standard game phase menus, images, button are already listed. There should not be anything in this file you need to modify nor change. "Why's that?", you ask! Because if you keep the same file names with your new artwork and graphics as presented in the boot.js file, everything just works. Do you remember reading in the Introduction Section:

Step 2: Create your standard game shell scenes.

> "If we create new graphics files, but call them by the same names we have in our game shell. We simply replace the game art with new art (with the same file names) and VOILA! NEW GAME ... same mechanics, same source code, yet with different "look & feel" – this is the secret sauce for cranking out a game per week."

- `init function` — prepares critical variables for game usage
- `preload function` — manages downloaded game assets.
- `create function` — manages the game re-size (min and max), alignment, and input.
- `enterIncorrectOrientation function` — notify gamer
- `leaveIncorrectOrientation function` — adjust game

NOTE: You can download this file from

http://makingbrowsergames.com/starterkits/dressup/v2_dressup_bootJS.pdf

Review this file; it is thoroughly annotated and documented to reduce the price of this pamphlet.

Preload.js

- `preload function` — manages game assets downloads
- `create function` — prepares a download bar and progress

This Game Phase manages our game assets downloads; you should optimize this process with the fewest possible downloads that are immediately required by your game. In smaller games – for example Menza Mental Math™ a Quizzes & Trivia –*, I "inline" the normal boot.js into the index.html and consolidated everything else into a game.js; doing so, deferred several potential downloaded files with this single combined file. Many developers use Browserify† to the same effect. The formal-style and separate preload.js now becomes a simple JavaScript object in a single web page application (SWPA) illustrated in the Introduction Section.

---

*http://makingbrowsergames.com/starterkits/quiz/game1/index.html
‡http://browserify.io

Step 2: Create your standard game shell scenes.

 NOTE: You can download this file from

http://makingbrowsergames.com/book/index11.html OR

http://makingbrowsergames.com/starterkits/dressup/v2_dressup_loadJS.pdf

Splash.js or Language.js

Modification to this file should be minimal as long as you have a standard menu system across all games. Loading the standard game phase menus, images, and buttons are already listed. There should not be anything in this file you need to modify nor change. However, if your game extensively uses text — such as hints, feedback, status changes or heads-up displays (HUD) — you may have considerable work to do.

You will discover tools such as PoEdit[*] or locize[†] beneficial in creating JSON files to substitute all text variables in the game. Both of these translation services allow you to edit your game's text into JSON format for i18next. The advantage of using such tools is that it's easier contract vendors to work on your translations.

Fortunately, there is a Phaser plugin[‡] we have adopted that works with i18next — an internationalization i18n-framework written in and for JavaScript —. This plugin allows us to have seamless translations in any of our games. It integrates i18next for translations management, which is widely adopted by the JS community at large in other projects as well.

Its Key features are:

- Support for translations namespaces;
- Simple key/value JSON;
- Seamless switching of languages;
- No extra function calls for translating strings, directly built into Phaser's Text object.

---

[*]https://poeditor.com/
[†]https://locize.com/
[‡]https://github.com/MakingBrowserGames/phaser-i18next

Step 2. Create your standard game shell scenes.   42

 Thanks for your patronage; here's a link to a significantly discounted price with access to all the bonus content or book bundles it provides: https://leanpub.com/LoRD/c/WDV3Q0dLe4v1

For our Mobile SWPA game, we use the `index.html` file. Review the `index.html` source code, and you find that the "splash scene" is merely a `div` tag using Bootstrap CSS.

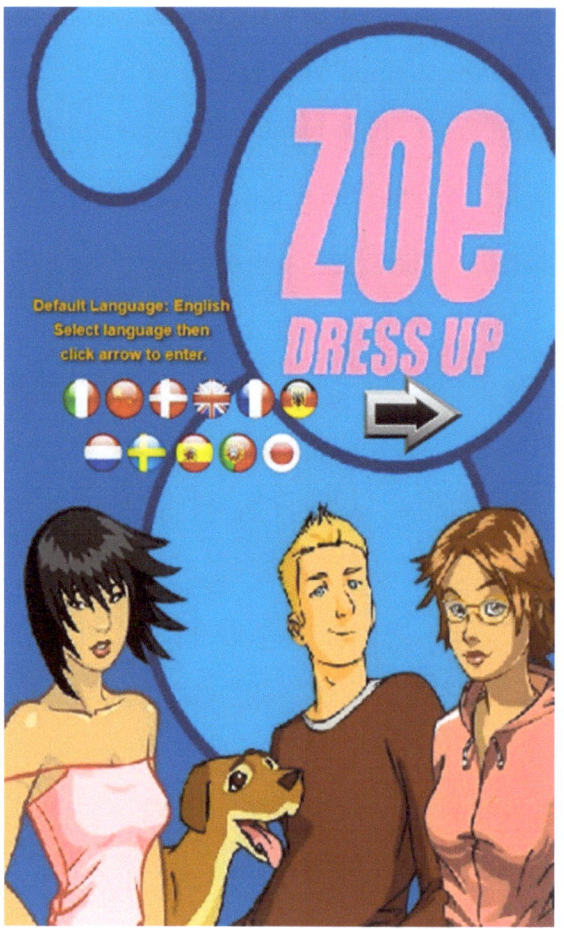

Language Selection for Zoe Dress-UP Game

NOTE: You can download this entire 5-page file from

http://makingbrowsergames.com/starterkits/dressup/v2_dressup_languageJS.pdf

For our Mobile SWPA, we use another `<div>` tag inside the `index.html` file. Review the mobile `index.html` source code, and you find that the "splash scene" is merely a "div" tag using Bootstrap

CSS.

 Here are some interesting facts* about the Internet and who is your "real" target audience.

Menu.js

Our next screen is the game's main menu. Normally, we divide our game into various levels of difficulty (depending on your game's genre and how you plan to implement it). However, Dress-Up Fashion games may not need or perhaps could combine the play phase within the main menu phase. In the *Phaser Game Design Workbook*†, I go into greater depth on workflow, how to load scripts (sync, async or deferred), and the use of internationalization (language selections).

Modification to this file should be minimal also so long as you have a standard menu system across all games. Loading the standard game phase menus, images, and buttons are already listed. There should not be anything in this file you need to modify nor change.

If you decide to have a separate main menu, you should offer your gamers several options before starting their game's play in earnest. The following scripts could be handled better as separate HTML web pages in a content management system (CMS) rather than stuffing everything into a Phaser Canvas. Remember the HTML5 canvas tag is merely a graphical display; it replaces the former Adobe Flash plugin in essence. Visit some of the other games on this book's website for examples of a content management system (CMS).

1. `preload function` — not used; everything was downloaded in the boot.js
2. `create function` — links downloaded assets for use during the game.
3. `beginGame function` — manages theme music
4. `gameCredits function` — manages theme music and game author information
5. `MoreGame function` — manages theme music, and provides access to more games from author

---

*http://www.internetworldstats.com/stats.htm
†https://leanpub.com/phaserjsgamedesignworkbook

Step 2: Create your standard game shell scenes.

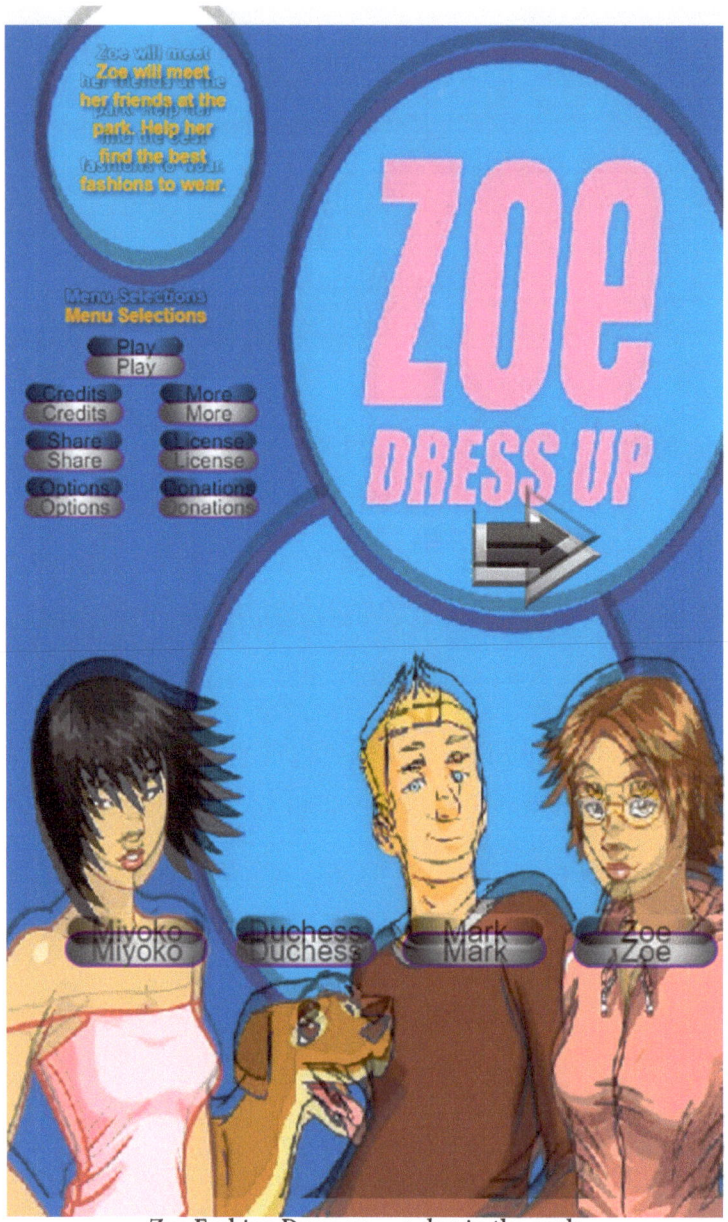

Zoe Fashion Dress up — a day in the park

 NOTE: You can download this file from

http://makingbrowsergames.com/starterkits/dressup/v2_dressup_menuJS.pdf

The following scripts are not included and would be better handled as separate HTML web pages in a content management system. Visit other games on the book's website for examples of a content management system (CMS).

Step 2: Create your standard game shell scenes.

- `About.js` — a page biography to enhance your portfolio and resume. In our mobile demonstration, the about page is used to enhance SEO and page content since it is simply another `<div>` tag.
- `Credits.js` — a page giving attributions.
- `Donations.js` — a page requesting financial support.
- `Instructions.js` or `help.js` — a page offering helpful hints, walk-throughs, achievement, awards, entitlements, or game rules. If the game instructions are minimal in content, it could be combined with another page.
- `Language.js` — a page offering gamers gameplay in their native language.
- `MoreGame.js` — a redirection page to your whole collection of games; used to build a loyal fan base.
- `Options.js` — a configuration page used to set keyboard input, and the like.
- `Scores.js` — pulls from a master database of recorded scores.
- `Share.js` — a page to enhance viral distribution of your game or announcements within the game. *See the twitter enhancement*.
- `SubmitScores.js` — collects and transmits of current game session for permanent storage.
- `wins.js` — records information into the gamer's registered account.
- `loose.js` — records information into the gamer's registered account.
- `WebMasters.js` — a page offering license and distribution information.

Play.js — Overview

Now let us dive straight into creating our game board, entities, and pieces. As you have seen, separating our code into these various files is a very good practice during the first developmental stages of our game.

Our demonstration games feature the ability to dress up various characters. Yes, we took the most difficult path. So to keep as much of the source code in a singular place for each avatar, each game level Play Phase, in which you can dress someone different, becomes its own separate play.js file. Our game was transpiled from [KiwiJS Game Design Workbook*](#) — the grandfather game framework of Phaser — into Phaser official and CE editions. I also re-structured its source code to take

---

*http://amzn.to/2Dni7bs

Step 2. Create your standard game shell scenes. 46

full advantages of Phaser's extraordinary features. Study the original KiwiJS Blueprint here*, and you find they had to "work around" several issues that are fully resolved for us in Phaser v2.x.x

The game Play phase holds both the core game logic about what to do if someone wants to save or print their creations and other essential functions for each character avatar. Let's study each character from the simplest to the most difficult.

Dog.js – a gentle introduction to standard Dress-UP games

 You can download this entire 4-page file from

http://makingbrowsergames.com/starterkits/dressup/v2_dressup_dogJS.pdf

Review this file; it is thoroughly annotated and documented to reduce the price of this pamphlet.

Play Game internal functions

1. Init function – not used
2. preload function – Lines 38 to 50
3. create function – Lines 51 to 130
4. update function – not used
5. render function – not used
6. changeFeature function – Lines 131 to 173

---

*http://www.kiwijs.org/2014/10/dressup-blueprint-updated/

Step 2. Create your standard game shell scenes.   47

```
26      "use strict";
27      var cfEyebrows;
28      //var cfHair;        //not used on dog
29      var cfEyes;
30      //var cfNose;        //not used on dog
31      //var cfGlasses;     //not used on dog
32      var cfMouth;
33   window.GAMEAPP.state.dog = {
34        init: function(){
37
38        preload: function(){
39            console.log(" %c Dog DressUP ", "color:white; background:red");
40
41            this.game.load.image('dog',
                  'assets/images/character/dog/outfit/base.png');
42
43            this.game.load.path = "assets/images/character/dog/";
44            this.load.spritesheet('eyebrows', 'eyebrows.png', 387, 472);
45            this.load.spritesheet('eyes', 'eyes.png', 406, 536);
46            this.load.spritesheet('mouth', 'mouth.png', 425, 727);
47            this.game.load.path ="";
48
49        },
50
```

Dog.js Preload — Lines 38 to 50

Nothing too special here; we're just creating a set of global variables to manage this scene's content and loading specific game assets for this scene.

Dog.js Create function – Lines 51 to 130

 You can download this entire 4-page file from

http://makingbrowsergames.com/starterkits/dressup/v2_dressup_dogJS.pdf

Review this file; it is thoroughly annotated and documented to reduce the price of this pamphlet.

- **Lines 51 to 63**: We are adding the game assets to the world stage, and setting some text information.

- **Lines 65 to 95**: The real work begins. We create an array data structure to hold the left heads-up display (HUD). This HUD is a column of buttons that manage the avatar customization. Zoe's pet dog – Duchess – only has 3 items to customize: the eyebrows, the eyes, and the mouth. Click the buttons will cycle through the sprite sheet. When we reach the last frame Phaser will automatically

Step 2: Create your standard game shell scenes.

return to the begin of the spriteSheet. We will assign a name to each HUD button. We will use its name to filter what actions to perform later.

- **Lines 96 to 130**: Creates and set-up a common menu available in every avatar scene. I could have consolidated these lines into one function call from each character, but for clarity, I broke the DRY rule (aka Don't Repeat Yourself). We will assign a name to each HUD button. This lower menu HUD are single click actions and do not manage a spriteSheet. We will use its name to filter what actions to perform later.

Dog.js create function – Lines 131 to 170

You can download this entire 4-page file from

http://makingbrowsergames.com/starterkits/dressup/v2_dressup_dogJS.pdf

Review this file; it is thoroughly annotated and documented to reduce the price of this pamphlet.

- **Lines 131 to 170** is a switch statement; it sorts clicks on which HUD button (cm0, cm1, and cm2). The left HUD buttons simply rotate through their assigned spriteSheets. The lower menu HUD manages various gaming options (mo0 to mo6). For example the "previous button" moves the game to the Miyoko avatar; the "next button" moves the game to the Mark avatar.
- **Lines 147 to 152** is the randomize button selection. I apologize for the hard coding but will give you a "homework" assignment to dynamically count the frames within a given spriteSheet and generate a random number to jump to that frame.
- **Lines 154 to 158** reset the dog features to their original values.

Mark.js = adding clothes and toggles

 You can download this entire 4-page file from

http://makingbrowsergames.com/starterkits/dressup/v2_dressup_markJS.pdf

Review this file; it is thoroughly annotated and documented to reduce the price of this pamphlet.

The "Mark Scene" adds clothing to the mix of buttons on the left HUD for a total of 4 buttons. The "clothing" button is merely a toggle that put his shirt on or takes it off. It is a simple process of making the clothes "visible" (or true; **see line 70, and 153 to 156**) or "invisible" (or false; ternary operations **found on lines 153 to 156**). In toggling, I prefer to use the ternary operation instead of an if/else; although the if/else statement is more readily apparent.

Miyoko.js = adding data structures and multiple spritesheets management

 You can download this entire 6-page file from

http://makingbrowsergames.com/starterkits/dressup/v2_dressup_miyokoJS.pdf

Review this file; it is thoroughly annotated and documented to reduce the price of this pamphlet.

The "Miyoko Scene" adds 2 more left HUD buttons into the mix for a total of 6 customization features. Let's study the complexity these buttons give in hopes you will avoid making these same mistakes.

Managing Hair and "Split-ends"

KiwiJS has several limitations unknown to the Phaser Community. Their "blueprint" provides a workaround to those limitations. When I transpiled their blueprint into Phaser, I restructured

Step 2. Create your standard game shell scenes.   50

everything except the artwork. Study the artwork provided for Miyoko, and you will find that her "hair" spriteSheets come in two flavors. I do not have an answer why the artist decided to provide two separate spriteSheets. If you study the files the hair-styles are split across the two files.

I decided to manage the two "hair" files with a toggle and an array — review lines 27 to 35. I load each file into an array — see lines 78 to 80.

In the `changeFeature` function (lines 158 to 176), I checked for which file (current hair array [0] or [1]) and used another Boolean to count the spriteSheet frames. If I discovered that I had run to the end of the first file (`frame >=8`; yes, it's hard-coded. Sorry!) then I toggled to the following file in the array. Turned the first file invisible, and made the second file visible.

Randomizing the hairstyles presents that same problem when choosing which file to use. I did not use DRY, but this could easily become a separate function call.

What's a Girl to Wear? Clothes management

The artist presents a different problem in the wardrobe. Instead of creating a single spriteSheet of all the clothing choices, they created separate files for each.

I chose to manage clothing items with an array and an index sentry. I would use the sentry to move to the various clothing stored in each array – see lines 33, 34. I added the clothes to the array in lines 67 to 71 and set their visibility.

In the `changeFeature` function (lines 185 to 196), I turned all the clothes invisible, increased the "current clothing count", and monitored whether I "over-ran" the end of the array. Now that I found the "current clothing", I made it visible.

Zoe.js – the full Monty

"The Full Monty?", is a British slang phrase of uncertain origin. It is generally used to mean "everything which is necessary, appropriate or possible; 'the works'". Similar North American

Step 2. Create your standard game shell scenes. 51

phrases include the whole kit and caboodle, the whole nine yards, the "whole ball of wax", the "whole enchilada", the "whole shebang", or [going] "whole hog". Whew!

You can download this entire 5-page file from

http://makingbrowsergames.com/starterkits/dressup/v2_dressup_zoeJS.pdf

Review this file; it is thoroughly annotated and documented to reduce the price of this pamphlet.

The "Zoe Scene" has 7 menu option on left HUD. After tackling the *"Kobayashi Maru* Miyoko" Scene*, Zoe becomes a "piece of cake".† The artist presents the same problem in the wardrobe as found in Miyoko. Instead of creating a single spriteSheet of all the clothing choices, they created separate files for each. So, we will use the same tactics to solve Zoe's wardrobe.

I chose to manage clothing items with an array and an index sentry. I would use the sentry to move to the various clothing store in each array — *see lines 33, 34*. I added the clothes to the array *in lines 70 to 78* and set their visibility. By now you have noticed that all the artwork set itself at X=0 and Y=0. This is the same positioning technique used in Jigsaw Puzzles, but that a topic in another book.

There are 5 clothing styles; it uses the same solution found in Miyoko — *see lines 183 to 195*. The randomization selection is nearly the same. I generate a random number and use that number as an index into the clothing array — *see lines 210 to 218*.

---
*https://en.wikipedia.org/wiki/Kobayashi_Maru
†https://idioms.thefreedictionary.com/piece+of+cake

8. Common Menus

Now for the *"secret sauce" of Dress-UP games*. If you followed our recommended readings above, you remember that in all four play scenes, I have avoided the **lower menu HUD print, save and camera snap-shot**. Let's study these now, but first let's understand why we should add these features into our *Dress-UP games*.

Naturally, Mattel was one of the first companies to start producing what tech and culture critic Justine Cassell refers to as ***"Pink Software,"*** games designed with stereotypical girly motifs. Mattel's first Barbie title was a dress-up game creatively named Barbie. The plot is this: Ken gives you a call and asks you out on a date; you then go shopping, picking situational garments appropriately. This design uses clothing as puzzle pieces, where a correct combination triggers a new puzzle. Barbie is bad for the same reasons most dress-up games are bad: you're simply slotting clothes onto a human figure thoughtlessly. : : :

Mattel got it right in 1996 with the Barbie Fashion Designer. Fashion Designer blurred the lines of virtual and physical dolls ***by allowing players to print their clothing creations***, enabled by special fabric sheets included with the game. To dress Barbie in the printed clothes, you had to cut and tape the templates together, much like traditional paper dolls. Even if players did not have a printer, Barbie would wear their custom designs in a 3D fashion show animation. The virtual fashion show was far superior to dressing physical Barbie in the printed garments, which were flimsy and *impractical outside of the game.* Unlike Barbie, there was no illusion of customization through matching situation-specific garments. Players edited the colors and patterns of the two-dimensional templates. Fashion Designer succeeded because clothing patterns were designed to be printed: players had control of the clothing itself, not just the clothing worn by a figure. : : :

The game was so successful it set new records for PC game sales at the time, churning out half a million copies in the first two months after it was released.

Read more here[a]

[a] https://killscreen.com/articles/awfulness-and-importance-dress-game/

```javascript
changeFeature: function(pointer){
    switch(pointer.name){
        case "cm0": //dog eye-browses
            console.log("cfEyebrows: "+cfEyebrows); //debug
            //Makes the element go to the next clothing item:
            cfEyebrows.frame += 1;
        break;
        case "cm1": //dog eyes
            cfEyes.frame += 1;
        break;
        case "cm2": //dog mouth
            cfMouth.frame += 1;
        break;
        case "mo0": //previous is Miyoko
            this.state.start("miyoko");
        break;
        case "mo1": //randomize
            //Loop elements and calls randomize method
            //TODO: HARDCODED needs a "dynamic solution"
            cfEyebrows.frame = Math.floor(Math.random() * 2);
            cfEyes.frame = Math.floor(Math.random() * 3);
            cfMouth.frame = Math.floor(Math.random() * 3);
        break;
        case "mo2": //reset; TODO remove hard coded variables
            //Loops through elements and set to 0
            cfEyebrows.frame = 0;
            cfEyes.frame = 0;
            cfMouth.frame = 0;
        break;
        case "mo3": //print; source code in chapter
        break;
        case "mo4": //snap-shot; source code in chapter
        break;
        case "mo5": //save; source code in chapter
        break;
        case "mo6": //next is Mark
            this.state.start("mark");
        break;
    }
}
```

Dress-UP commands' engine

So, let's add the printing, saving and camera snap-shot features to our game. *I redesigned the original blueprint.* There was no practical reason to take the gamer to a separate "print, save, snap-shot" page when in reality (behind those displays) we're simply making the various HUDs invisible.

Printing

We have several options available to us for printing. The simplest is using the native window.print() capabilities. The window.print() opens a "Print Dialog Box" which lets our gamer choose their printing options for the current browser window.

```
// ============================================================
// --------------------------------------------
// Supporting game print
// --------------------------------------------
// ============================================================
// Print menu option calls a media preparation functions.
case "mo3":         //print; source code does not appear online!
        this.prepMedia();

    break;

// Simplest option
printScene: function(){
        this.printBtn.visible = false;
        window.focus();         // required for IE
        window.print();
        // return to Main Menu after printing or cancelled print job.
        this.state.start("menu");
},

prepMedia: function(){
        //used to clear HUD buttons for print and camera snap-shot
        this.cmBtn[0].visible = false;
        this.cmBtn[1].visible = false;
        this.cmBtn[2].visible = false;
        this.cmBtn[3].visible = false;
        this.cmBtn[4].visible = false;
```

```
28              this.cmBtn[5].visible = false;
29              this.cmBtn[6].visible = false;
30              this.moBtn[0].visible = false;
31              this.moBtn[1].visible = false;
32              this.moBtn[2].visible = false;
33              this.moBtn[3].visible = false;
34              this.moBtn[4].visible = false;
35              this.moBtn[5].visible = false;
36              // New button for post-rendering
37              this.printBtn = this.game.add.button(
38                  this.world.centerX,
39                  this.world.height-100,
40                  "printBtn",
41                  this.printScene,
42                  this,
43                  0, 1, 0, 1);
44              //moBtn[6].visible = false;
45          },
```

As simple as this all appears, there are some problems. The website http://caniuse.com suggests using `window.matchMedia('print')` where possible. MDN web docs states:

- Starting with Chrome 46.0 this method is blocked inside an `<iframe>` unless its sandbox attribute has the value allow-modals. The `<iframe>` is a hidden object, and content is duplicated into it.

- You can study a variety of more sophisticated print methods here.

Saving

We need to determine what our gamers will save, where to save the information, and how to store the information. For a simple Dress-Up game, we can use something called `local.storage` which is a mechanism available in the browser window. It will store data with no expirations. Our games can store up to 5MB in their browsers as "key/value" pairs, and that information is never transferred to our server. Furthermore, this storage is "per domain origin" meaning that all the gaming pages we serve our gamers, from one origin, are available.

Local storage is outside of the Phaser canvas and a featured capability of the browser window. So before we activate it, we should determine if it is available in their browser.

```javascript
// ================================================================
// ----------------------------------------
// Supporting game save
// These functions are used for storing and changing
// cookies or localStorage in the site.  The variable functions
// use these.
// ----------------------------------------
// ================================================================
function UseStorage()
{
    var storageDefined = false;
    // Wrap into a "try catch" for work-around in Firefox bugs:
    try
    {
        if (typeof (localStorage) != "undefined")
        {
            storageDefined = true;
        }
    }
    catch (ex)
    {

    }
    return storageDefined;
}
// This function creates a cookie or localStorage (if necessary)
//       and sets its (string) value
function SetStorageString(name, value)
{
    delim = gDefDelim;
    if (typeof (gameDelim) != "undefined")
    {
        //set GAMEAPP.gameDelim to your unique game SKU
        delim = GAMEAPP.gameDelim;
    }
    if (UseStorage())
    {
        localStorage.setItem(name + delim, String(value));
    }else{
        //Set a cookie text
        var days = 365; // Number of days to keep the cookies
        var expires = new Date();
        expires.setTime(expires.getTime()
```

```
                            + (days * 24 * 60 * 60 * 1000));
            document.cookie = name + delim + "=" + value + "; path=/"
                            + ((expires == null) ? "" : "; expires="
                            + expires.toGMTString());
        }
    }
    // Store
    localStorage.setItem("avatar", "Zoe");
    localStorage.setItem("Eyebrows", cfEyebrows.frame);
    localStorage.setItem("Hair", cfHair.frame);
    localStorage.setItem("Eyes", cfEyes.frame);
    localStorage.setItem("Nose", cfNose.frame);
    localStorage.setItem("Glasses", cfGlasses.frame);
    localStorage.setItem("Mouth", cfMouth.frame);

    // Retrieve
    // This function reads the cookie or localStorage and returns
    //   its value as a string.
    function ReadStorageString(name)
    {
        delim = GAMEAPP.gameDelim;
        if (typeof (GAMEAPP.gameDelim) != "undefined")
        {
            delim = GAMEAPP.gameDelim;
        }
        var val = "";
        if (UseStorage())
        {
            var temp = String(localStorage.getItem(name + delim));
            if (temp != "null")
            {
                val = temp;
            }
        }else{
            var fullName = name + delim + "=";
            var strings = document.cookie.split(';');
            for (var i = 0; i < strings.length; i++)
            {
                var str = strings[i];
                while (str.charAt(0) == ' ')
                {
                    str = str.substring(1, str.length);
                }
```

```
 87
 88                                if (str.indexOf(fullName) == 0)
 89                                {
 90                                        val = str.substring(fullName.length, str.length);
 91                                        break;
 92                                }
 93                        }
 94                }
 95                return val;
 96        }
```

As easy as this all appears, there are some problems. The website http://caniuse.com lists current known issues and provides resources for further investigation. MDN web docs state:

- From Firefox 45 onwards, when the browser crashes/restarts, the amount of data saved per origin *is limited to 10MB*. This has been done to avoid memory issues caused by excessive usage of web storage.

 - Access to Web Storage from third-party IFrames is denied if the user has *disabled third-party cookies*[*] (Firefox implements this behavior from version 43 onwards.)

 - Web Storage is not the same as mozStorage[†] (Mozilla's XPCOM interfaces to SQLite) or the Session store API[‡] (an XPCOM storage utility for use by extensions).

 - The issue with a gamer using browser "incognito" modes. I recommend a side-trip to read this comprehensive article — *Private browsing vs. Storage and Databases.*[§]

Camera Snap-shots

Let's not make this overly complicated. The gamer's desktop device has a "Print Scene" capabilities. What we need to do is clear off the menu HUDs.

The function would make all the HUD buttons invisible and provide another small button that would return to normal visible operations. Research through the source code for examples on turning items "invisible". A sample function might follow as this

---

[*]https://support.mozilla.org/en-US/kb/disable-third-party-cookies
[†]https://developer.mozilla.org/en-US/docs/Storage
[‡]https://developer.mozilla.org/en-US/docs/Session_store_API
[§]https://blog.whatwg.org/tag/localstorage

```
// ============================================================
// --------------------------------------------
// Supporting game Print Screen
// --------------------------------------------
// ============================================================
// Print menu option calls a media preparation functions.
case "mo4":          //print; source code does not appear online!
        this.prepMedia();
break;

prepMedia: function(){
        //used to clear HUD buttons for print and camera snap-shot
        this.cmBtn[0].visible = false;
        this.cmBtn[1].visible = false;
        this.cmBtn[2].visible = false;
        this.cmBtn[3].visible = false;
        this.cmBtn[4].visible = false;
        this.cmBtn[5].visible = false;
        this.cmBtn[6].visible = false;
        this.moBtn[0].visible = false;
        this.moBtn[1].visible = false;
        this.moBtn[2].visible = false;
        this.moBtn[3].visible = false;
        this.moBtn[4].visible = false;
        this.moBtn[5].visible = false;
        //Leave the "next" button visible to return to normal operations
        //m0Btn[6].visible = false;
}
```

Perhaps, you might want more control over what your gamers take "snap-shot" from your game. There is a method to capture just the html5 canvas in its current rendering; it is not for the "faint of heart".*

---

*https://www.collinsdictionary.com/us/dictionary/english/not-for-the-faint-hearted

```javascript
//assuming your game is inside a div calle phaserCanvas
var clickToSave= document.getElementById('phaserCanvas');

function saveCanvas(link, filename) {
    link.href = game.canvas.toDataURL();
    link.download = filename;
};
clickToSave.onclick = function(){
    //create an image object
    var name = "name."+"png";
    //send new image to the process function
    saveCanvas(this, name);

};
```

9. Conclusion

We are at the end of game development and should deploy our game into the wild. Topics such as launch times, download times, time to first byte (TTFB)[*], domain naming servers (DNS) lookups; all these now come into our business project's scope.

When you launch your final "Golden Release"[†], it is critical that we "collapse" all these module files into as few as possible, obfuscate[‡] them and minify them using Browserify[§]. I recommend several of these tools found in the reference workbooks. "How to use such tools?", you say? Take a side-trip to this fantastic article.[¶] But you could also "copy-paste", ensuring all the dependency are in the correct sequence.

More Game Starter Kit Tutorials

NOTE: This tutorial is a single chapter from a larger collection of game mechanies for both Phaser v2 and v3 found on http://leanpub.com/pgskc/ You can find all these Game Starter Kits for Phaser v2 and Game Starter Kits for Phaser v3 on Amazon.com. Search for Stephen Gose Phaser

Further Information

For those seeking more information about game design, ludology, gaming theory, mechanisms, and mechanics, there are references to these throughout this series of books. Information Technology is always a "moving target"; so I have provided a website with the most updated information, code corrections, and software updates.

---

[*]https://blog.cloudflare.com/ttfb-time-to-first-byte-considered-meaningles/
[†]http://www.webopedia.com/TERM/G/gold_version.html
[‡]https://en.wikipedia.org/wiki/Obfuscation
[§]http://browserify.io
[¶]https://medium.freecodecamp.org/javascript-modules-part-2-module-bundling-5020383cf306

http://makingbrowsergames.com/

Introduction References

Let's conclude this chapter with related resource references available through LeanPub* and Amazon International†.

- Supporting website and bonus content: http://makingbrowsergames.com/starterkits/

- Game Design Workbook (LeanPub)‡ or from Amazon Paperback§ or Kindle / mobi / epub editon¶,

 - Phaser Game Prototypes (LeanPub)‖ or coming soon to Amazon**,

 - Phaser Game Development Library (Bundled offer by LeanPub)††,

 - Ultimate Phaser Library (Bundled offer by LeanPub)‡‡

 - Individual Phaser Game Startkit chapters from Amazon for Kindle§§ or Amazon International Paperback¶¶.

---

*https://leanpub.com/u/pbmcube
†https://www.amazon.com/s/ref=nb_sb_noss_2?url=search-alias%3Daps&field-keywords=stephen+gose
‡https://leanpub.com/phaserjsgamedesignworkbook
§http://amzn.to/2eXtUX4
¶http://amzn.to/2xXk7oP
‖https://leanpub.com/LoRD
**http://makingbrowsergames.com/book/
††https://leanpub.com/b/phasergamedevelopment
‡‡https://leanpub.com/b/ultimatephaserlibrary
§§http://amzn.to/2fci20g
¶¶http://amzn.to/2gV5CtJ

Copyright © 1972-2017, Stephen Gose. All rights reserved.

www.ingramcontent.com/pod-product-compliance
Lightning Source LLC
Chambersburg PA
CBHW051918210526
45473CB00006B/2056